THE SOLAR SYSTEM
PLUTO

A MyReportLinks.com Book

KIM A. O'CONNELL

MyReportLinks.com Books

an imprint of

 Enslow Publishers, Inc.

Box 398, 40 Industrial Road
Berkeley Heights, NJ 07922
USA

MyReportLinks.com Books, an imprint of Enslow Publishers, Inc. MyReportLinks® is a registered trademark of Enslow Publishers, Inc.

Library of Congress Cataloging-in-Publication Data

O'Connell, Kim A.
  Pluto / Kim A. O'Connell.
    p. cm. — (The solar system)
  Includes bibliographical references and index.
  ISBN 0-7660-5210-9
  1. Pluto (Planet)—Juvenile literature. I. Title. II. Solar system (Berkeley Heights, N.J.)
  QB701.O26 2005
  523.482—dc22
                            2004023132

Printed in the United States of America

10 9 8 7 6 5 4 3 2 1

To Our Readers:
Through the purchase of this book, you and your library gain access to the Report Links that specifically back up this book.

The Publisher will provide access to the Report Links that back up this book and will keep these Report Links up to date on **www.myreportlinks.com** for five years from the book's first publication date.

We have done our best to make sure all Internet addresses in this book were active and appropriate when we went to press. However, the author and the Publisher have no control over, and assume no liability for, the material available on those Internet sites or on other Web sites they may link to.

The usage of the MyReportLinks.com Books Web site is subject to the terms and conditions stated on the Usage Policy Statement on **www.myreportlinks.com**.

A password may be required to access the Report Links that back up this book. The password is found on the bottom of page 4 of this book.

Any comments or suggestions can be sent by e-mail to comments@myreportlinks.com or to the address on the back cover.

MyReportLinks.com Books
Great Books, Great Links, Great for Research!

The Internet sites listed on the next four pages can save you hours of research time. These Internet sites—we call them "Report Links"—are constantly changing, but we keep them up to date on our Web site.

Give it a try! Type http://www.myreportlinks.com into your browser, click on the series title, then the book title, and scroll down to the Report Links listed for this book.

The Report Links will bring you to great source documents, photographs, and illustrations. MyReportLinks.com Books save you time, feature Report Links that are kept up to date, and make report writing easier than ever!

Please see "To Our Readers" on the copyright page for important information about this book, the MyReportLinks.com Web site, and the Report Links that back up this book.

Please enter **PPL1369** if asked for a password.

Report Links

The Internet sites described below can be accessed at http://www.myreportlinks.com

*EDITOR'S CHOICE

Solar System Exploration: Pluto
Discover Pluto and its moon when you visit this NASA site. Several of the best images of Pluto, the least explored planet, are offered here.

*EDITOR'S CHOICE

▶Pluto: Your Travel Guide to the Solar System
This BBC science site provides information on what weather conditions are like on Pluto, the coldest planet in the solar system. Information is also available on its history and unusual features.

*EDITOR'S CHOICE

Clyde W. Tombaugh
On February 18, 1930, Clyde W. Tombaugh discovered the planet Pluto while working at the Lowell Observatory in Flagstaff, Arizona. Learn more about his life on this New Mexico Museum of Space History site.

*EDITOR'S CHOICE

▶New Horizons: Shedding Light on Frontier Worlds
Scheduled to launch in January 2006, the New Horizons mission to Pluto, Charon, and the Kuiper Belt will travel past Jupiter to take advantage of its gravity to slingshot the spacecraft into the outer solar system. Learn more at this site.

*EDITOR'S CHOICE

▶Twenty-fifth Anniversary of the Discovery of Pluto's Moon, Charon
James W. Christy of the U.S. Naval Observatory discovered Pluto's moon, later named Charon, on June 22, 1978. Learn about his discovery from this Web site.

*EDITOR'S CHOICE

▶Windows to the Universe: Pluto
This comprehensive Web site takes a look at Pluto's composition, atmosphere, and the mythological basis of its name and offers links to many other sites about the ninth planet.

Report Links

▶ Charon

In Greek mythology, Charon ferried the souls of the dead across the river Styx to the underworld ruled by Pluto, also called Hades. Learn more about the mythological Charon from this site.

▶ A Cold New World

The discovery of Quaoar, a large Kuiper Belt Object, is discussed in this NASA science article. Quaoar is one of the largest objects to be discovered past Pluto.

▶ Exploring the Planets: Pluto

This National Air and Space Museum site on Pluto offers information on the planet's unusual orbit, its satellite, Charon, and more. Images are also included.

▶ Journey to the Farthest Planet

Dr. Alan Stern is the principal investigator of the New Horizons mission that will study Pluto, Charon, and several Kuiper Belt Objects. This *Scientific American* article is his first-hand account of the project.

▶ The Kuiper Belt

The Kuiper Belt is named for the famous Dutch-American astronomer Gerard Kuiper, considered the father of modern planetary science, who suggested its existence in 1951. This site describes the disk-shaped region of icy bodies beyond Neptune.

▶ Lowell Observatory

Percival Lowell spent much of the last years of his life looking for "Planet X." On February 18, 1930, Clyde Tombaugh found the planet that would later be known as Pluto. Read about the observatory that Percival Lowell built and the other discoveries made there.

▶ National Maritime Museum: Pluto

This National Maritime Museum Web site for Pluto provides a look at the planet's discovery in 1930. Information on its unusual orbit is included.

▶ National Space Science Data Center: Pluto

Basic facts and information on the New Horizons mission to Pluto are provided on this NASA site. A gallery of Pluto photographs is also available.

Any comments? Contact us: **comments@myreportlinks.com**

Report Links

The Internet sites described below can be accessed at http://www.myreportlinks.com

New Horizons Over Mysterious Pluto

This comprehensive site on Pluto will provide you with information on its discovery, moon, size, unusual orbit, atmosphere, and the many reasons why we should explore Pluto now.

New World Found Beyond Pluto

From this site, learn about the discovery of Quaoar, the largest object to be found in the solar system's Kuiper Belt. Information on the discovery of the first Kuiper Belt Object in 1992 is also available.

Nineplanets.org: Pluto

Although Pluto is still officially considered a planet, many astronomers believe that Pluto is an icy Kuiper Belt Object. At this site, learn why.

The Planet Pluto

This academic Web site offers a comprehensive look at the ninth planet, some images of Pluto, and links to more information about the planet.

The Planets—Pluto

Pluto is a very cold planet thought to be made primarily of ice and rock. The planet also has polar caps and experiences snowstorms. Read more about its weather on this BBC site.

Pluto

Pluto, the farthest planet from the Sun, is the only one in our solar system not yet visited by a spacecraft. Find out more about Pluto on this Web site.

Pluto: Clearest View

Because Pluto is so far away, few pictures exist of it. Even with a fairly large telescope, it is difficult to observe the planet. At this site, you will see one of the best images ever taken of Pluto and its moon, Charon.

Pluto: Planet or Not?

This Ontario Science Center site presents evidence for why Pluto should be considered a planet, and evidence for why Pluto should not be considered a planet. Read the arguments, and submit your vote.

Report Links

The Internet sites described below can be accessed at http://www.myreportlinks.com

▶**Pluto, the Ninth Planet**

Written by an astronomer from Lowell Observatory, this site about Pluto offers a tour of the phases of Charon, Pluto's moon, and an explanation why Pluto is really a planet.

▶**Pluto Fact Sheet**

This NASA site for Pluto provides a large number of statistics for the planet, including an Earth/Pluto comparison chart. Information on Charon, Pluto's moon, is also provided.

▶**Pluto Portal**

This site was developed by NASA's principal investigator for the New Horizons mission to Pluto and beyond, which is set to launch in January 2006. Learn more about the planet, the mission, and the pioneering scientists involved.

▶**Pluto's Atmosphere Is Expanding, Researchers Say**

Scientists have found that Pluto is slowly moving away from the Sun. But instead of this producing a drop in atmospheric pressure, the pressure of Pluto's atmosphere has doubled. Read more about this interesting discovery in an MIT article.

▶**Pushing the Envelope on the Solar System's 'Wild West' Frontiers**

The principal investigator for the New Horizons mission to Pluto is Alan Stern, a planetary scientist and astrophysicist. At this site, find out why he thinks we need to send a spacecraft to Pluto and the Kuiper Belt.

▶**Race Against Time: Long Road to Pluto and Why We're Going**

The New Horizons Mission will fly by Pluto and its moon, Charon, and then continue on through the Kuiper Belt. Images and data will be transmitted back to Earth. Learn more about the project on this site.

▶**The Struggles to Find the Ninth Planet**

On this site, you can read Clyde Tombaugh's account of the difficulties he faced in the search for Planet X, which led to his discovery of Pluto in 1930.

▶**Where the Sun and Ice Worlds Meet**

On this NASA Web site, you can read about the Solar Wind Around Pluto (SWAP) instrument that will be part of the New Horizons mission to the planet. This instrument will measure interactions with the solar wind, a stream of particles emitted by the Sun.

Pluto Facts

Age
Approximately 4.5 billion years

Diameter
1,468 miles (2,370 kilometers)

Composition
Probably a rock-ice core; water-ice mantle; crust of frozen methane

Average Distance From the Sun
3.7 billion miles (5.9 billion kilometers)

Average Distance From Earth
3.58 billion miles (5.76 billion kilometers)

Orbital Period (year, in Earth years)
248 years

Rotational Period (day, in Earth days)
6.39 days

Mass
0.25 percent of Earth's mass

Temperature
May be as low as −350°F (−212°C) at surface, perhaps even colder in certain sections

Surface Gravity
7 percent of Earth's gravity

Chapter 1

The Man Who Found Planet X

During the nineteenth century, astronomers noticed that the planet Uranus, the seventh planet from the Sun, seemed to be acting a bit strangely. Something with a fairly strong gravitational pull seemed to be tugging on the planet, moving its orbit out of its expected path. When Uranus's neighbor Neptune was discovered in 1846, that discovery seemed to explain the gravitational pull. But astronomers soon noticed that something else was out there, exerting a gravitational force on both Uranus and Neptune. By the turn of the twentieth century, the search was on for a yet-unidentified planet beyond the eight known planets of the solar system.

▷ Lowell's Quest

In 1905, an astronomer named Percival Lowell became determined to find this Planet X, as he called the mysterious outer planet. In 1894, Lowell, a Harvard graduate from a prestigious New England family, had founded a private observatory that bore his name in Flagstaff, Arizona, where he spent most of his time studying Mars. (He was one of the early believers in the existence of intelligent life on Mars.)

But Lowell turned his telescope toward the farthest reaches of the solar system whenever he could, searching for Planet X. The search was not an easy one, however. An astronomer has to know where in the vast sky to start looking for a new planet—otherwise, it is a long process of trial and error. If the general location is known, then that section of the sky must be watched carefully for days at a time. Sometimes, the rocky space objects known as asteroids can appear as faint, moving specks, sending astronomers

"One day with life and heart is more than time enough to find a world." Lowell

△ Percival Lowell founded the Lowell Observatory, where Pluto's discovery would take place.

on a wild goose chase for a planet where there is none. Lowell had predicted a position where Planet X should be found, but he was not able to find it, although his quest continued until his death, in 1916.

▷ An Astronomer's Beginnings

But where the well-educated Lowell had failed, a self-taught astronomer would succeed. In 1918, a twelve-year-old farm boy from Illinois named Clyde Tombaugh, whose family later moved to another farm in Kansas, was loaned a small telescope by his uncle. As soon as he tilted the scope toward the sky, Tombaugh became hooked on astronomy. He bought his first telescope from

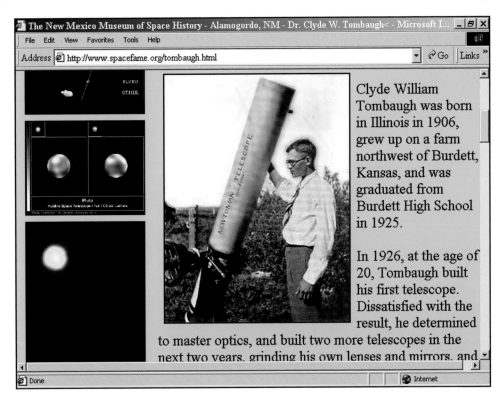

The New Mexico Museum of Space History - Alamogordo, NM - Dr. Clyde W. Tombaugh< - Microsoft I...

File   Edit   View   Favorites   Tools   Help

Address http://www.spacefame.org/tombaugh.html   Go   Links

Clyde William Tombaugh was born in Illinois in 1906, grew up on a farm northwest of Burdett, Kansas, and was graduated from Burdett High School in 1925.

In 1926, at the age of 20, Tombaugh built his first telescope. Dissatisfied with the result, he determined to master optics, and built two more telescopes in the next two years, grinding his own lenses and mirrors, and

Done   Internet

▲ Clyde Tombaugh was a self-taught astronomer when he was hired to work at Lowell to continue the search for Planet X.

Sears, but was unhappy with it so he decided to build one of his own in 1925. His father took a second job to help pay for the materials his son needed to build it. It was the first of more than thirty telescopes that Clyde Tombaugh would build during his lifetime.

In 1928, he built a nine-inch (twenty-three-centimeter) telescope, which he used to observe the planets and stars. Tombaugh used things he found on the farm to craft this telescope: a cream separator to make part of the telescope's base and a piece of the crankshaft from his father's 1910 Buick for another part.[1] By the time he was twenty-two, only ten years after he had first held a telescope, Tombaugh had made detailed sketches of the surfaces of planets. He sent his drawings of Jupiter and Mars to the astronomers at the Lowell Observatory, hoping only to have them offer advice. What they did instead was offer the amateur astronomer without a college degree a job at Lowell. In that position, Clyde Tombaugh would soon make astronomical history.

Tombaugh's Great Discovery

In 1929, Clyde Tombaugh was hired by the Lowell Observatory to continue the search for Planet X begun by Percival Lowell.

△ Clyde Tombaugh's painstaking search of the sky yielded historic results on February 18, 1930, when he discovered Pluto. Tombaugh is pictured with the telescope he used to find the planet.

Tombaugh's job was to take photographs of a small part of the sky where the unknown planet was predicted to be. Pairs of photographs, taken several nights apart, would then be developed on photographic glass plates and the plates examined through a blink microscope. What Tombaugh was looking for was the motion of a planet as revealed against a background of stars over time. If the images showed a celestial body jumping around compared to the surrounding stars, it just might be a new planet. Looking at photograph after photograph was a tedious job, however. Tombaugh had to sift through hundreds of thousands of pairs of star images.[2]

Tombaugh decided that Lowell's predictions for Planet X's location were not reliable. And so he began his search of the entire sky, section by section. He examined up to thirty-five thousand stars a day, and he also found a comet and many asteroids. "I wasn't even sure there was a Planet X," he recalled later.

After ten tedious months of searching, his patience and painstaking work paid off. On February 18, 1930, Tombaugh found what he had been looking for in the constellation of Gemini—Planet X. When he realized his discovery, he said, "It made my day. . . . For 45 minutes I was the only person in the world who knew the position of Planet X."[3]

Tombaugh's discovery at age twenty-four was an even more impressive achievement since the predicted positions of Planet X had not really helped him in his search. His discovery of the ninth planet in the solar system was found through his own incredibly detailed work. The staff of the observatory spent several weeks verifying Tombaugh's find, so it was not until March 13 that the new planet was announced to the world as Pluto. The date also happened to mark the seventy-fifth birthday of Percival Lowell.

▷ A Shadowy Figure in Space

This planet, the most distant planet from the Sun, was named Pluto for the god of the underworld—a shadowy figure in mythology and a shadowy figure in space. In Greek mythology,

Pluto was the brother of Zeus and Poseidon (Jupiter and Neptune in Roman mythology), so the name seemed to fit, as the planet officially joined its planetary siblings. Other names had been suggested for the planet. They included names from mythology—*Artemis, Atlas, Bacchus, Minerva,* and *Zeus*—as well as *Lowell,* to honor the late astronomer, and *Constance,* to honor his widow. Constance Lowell visited Clyde Tombaugh at the observatory in the summer of 1930 and, as later recalled by the discoverer of Pluto, is claimed to have said that she was eager to meet the man who had found her "husband's planet."[4] After Pluto was discovered, astronomers realized that the gravitational oddness of Uranus and Neptune was actually the result of inaccurate measurements of the outer planets, which were quickly corrected.

APOD: February 4, 1997 - Clyde W. Tombaugh: 1906-1997 - Microsoft Internet Explorer

File   Edit   View   Favorites   Tools   Help

Address   http://antwrp.gsfc.nasa.gov/apod/ap970204.html

Clyde W. Tombaugh: 1906-1997
Credit and Copyright: J. Kelly Beatty

Explanation: Astronomer Clyde Tombaugh, discoverer of Pluto, died on January 17th. Inspiring many during his long and exceptional career, he had been living in Las Cruces,

Tombaugh is pictured with the nine-inch telescope he built from discarded farm materials when he was a young man.

A Distinguished Career

While Clyde Tombaugh continued working at Lowell for the next thirteen years, he also attended college on a scholarship from the University of Kansas, went on to earn his master's degree in astronomy there, and married Patricia Edson. He taught at several universities, worked in ballistics research, and in 1955 founded the astronomy research program at New Mexico State University. While the discovery of Pluto was undoubtedly his most famous achievement, Clyde Tombaugh also discovered six star clusters, two comets, a couple dozen galaxy clusters, one supercluster, and hundreds of asteroids in his long and illustrious career. When the Smithsonian Institution asked Tombaugh if it could have the nine-inch (twenty-three-centimeter) telescope he had made in 1928, as he later recounted to an interviewer, "I told them I was still using it."[5] He remained an active stargazer until he died, at age ninety, on January 17, 1997.

Pluto's Unexpected Moon

For years following Tombaugh's discovery of Pluto, little was known about the most distant planet in the solar system. In the 1970s, however, an astronomer named James Christy noticed that Pluto appeared to have a faint bulge on one side of its perimeter. The bulge also seemed to change position.

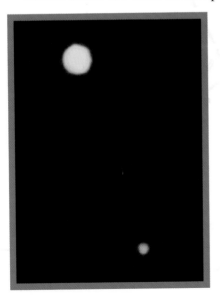

The Hubble Space Telescope captured this view of Pluto and Charon in 1994 when Pluto was 2.6 billion miles (4.4 billion kilometers) from Earth.

Christy concluded that the moving bump was actually a moon. It was named Charon, after the mythological boatman who ferried the souls of the dead to the underworld ruled by Pluto. Charon, about half the size of Pluto, is the largest satellite in the solar system in relation to its host planet. In fact, Pluto and Charon are so close in size and move in such a close and similar pattern that the two are sometimes known as a binary, or double, planet.

Planet or Not?

Not everyone thinks that Pluto-Charon make up a binary planet, however. Some do not even consider Pluto a planet at all. Early in the 1990s, scientists discovered a distant region of icy debris beyond Neptune that is now known as the Kuiper Belt. Named for the Dutch-American astronomer Gerard Kuiper, considered the father of modern planetary science, this disk-shaped region is thought of as the final frontier in our solar system. It is filled with what scientists estimate may be tens of thousands of icy bodies smaller than planets. These bodies are known as Kuiper Belt Objects (KBOs), although only about five hundred have been identified so far. These objects, 7.5 billion to 9.3 billion miles (12 to 15 billion kilometers) away from the Sun, may be "leftovers" from the planet-building process. In 2002, scientists discovered a KBO beyond Pluto, named Quaoar (pronounced KWAH-whar), which is orbiting the Sun in a near-perfect circular orbit.

Because Pluto and Charon are so small and seem to share many of the same properties as KBOs, some astronomers now consider Pluto a Kuiper Belt Object rather than a planet. The Rose Center for Earth and Space, part of the American Museum of Natural History in New York City, was the first major public institution to stop referring to Pluto as a planet in its exhibits. But the International Astronomical Union, which is the official naming organization for planets and other bodies, still considers Pluto a planet, at least for the time being.

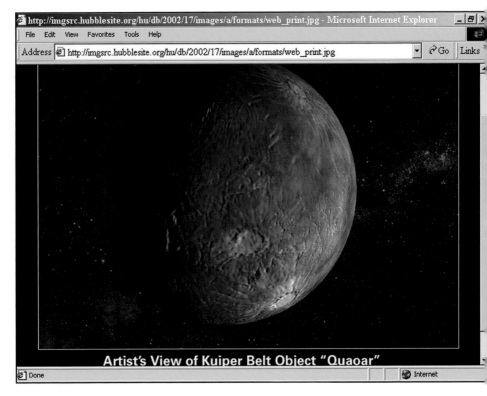

Artist's View of Kuiper Belt Object "Quaoar"

△ *How big does a body in space have to be to be considered a planet? Astronomers disagree on the answer, but Quaoar, a KBO orbiting beyond Pluto, is not that much smaller than the ninth planet in the solar system.*

▷ With Pluto, Expect the Unexpected

From the search for Planet X to the discovery of Charon, Pluto has always surprised astronomers with something they were not expecting. The November 2004 discovery that a distant Kuiper Belt Object known as 2002 AW197 is smaller than was previously thought may just help Pluto keep its designation as a planet after all.

University of Arizona astronomer John Stansberry and his colleagues have been able to determine the size of KBOs more accurately by getting better data on how reflective these icy objects are. Their data came from the Multiband Imaging Photometer

An artist's conception of the Spitzer Space Telescope as it left Earth soon after its launch on August 25, 2003.

on Spitzer (MIPS). *Spitzer* refers to the Spitzer Space Telescope, which was launched in 2003.

The MIPS instrument detected heat from 2002 AW197, more than 4 billion miles (6 billion kilometers) away, which gave scientists a different idea of the KBO's reflectivity and thus its size. According to Stansberry, "2002 AW197 is believed to be one of the largest KBOs thus far discovered. These results indicate that this object is larger than all but one main-belt asteroid (Ceres), about half the size of Pluto's moon, Charon, and about 30 percent as large and a tenth as massive as Pluto. . . ."[6]

By learning more about the KBOs, astronomers can learn more about the ninth planet. As Stansberry said, "We're finally starting to get data on the basic physical parameters of KBOs . . . That will help us determine what their compositions are, how they evolve, how massive they are, what their real size distributions and dynamics are and how Pluto fits into the whole picture."[7]

Chapter 2 ▶

The Most Distant Planet

Pluto's discovery by Clyde Tombaugh in 1930 made it the only planet to be discovered in modern times.[1] Since most of the solar system's planets had been known to humans for thousands of years, the discovery of a new planet was an historic event. Although more than seventy-five years have passed since its discovery, much about Pluto remains a mystery to astronomers.

▷ Theories About Pluto's Beginnings

Some astronomers thought that Pluto was a "lost moon" of Neptune. Pluto closely resembles Triton, Neptune's largest moon, in size, temperature, and density. Originally, it was thought that Pluto and Triton might have had some kind of encounter that sent Pluto out into its present orbit. Other astronomers believed that Pluto was created in the swirling mass of solar material that also created the other planets. Although some astronomers have

△ The planets of the solar system are arranged in order of their distance from the Sun, at left, and are shown in sizes relative to each other. Here, tiny Pluto looks like a speck at the edge of the solar system.

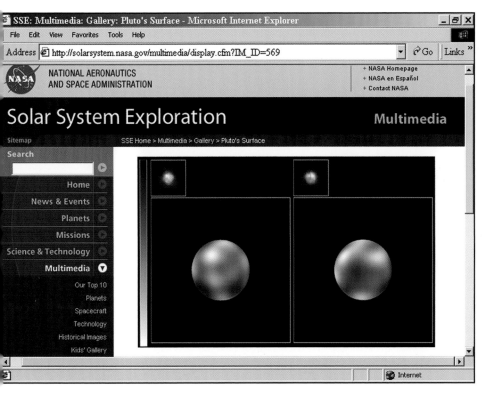

▲ *These images of opposite hemispheres on Pluto were taken by a camera aboard the Hubble Space Telescope. They were the first to offer variations in brightness, which scientists think may offer clues to the surface features of Pluto. The small images at the top are actual images; the bottom pictures are processed versions of several Hubble observations.*

reasoned that Charon was created in the same way, a popular theory is that Charon was the fallout of a massive collision between Pluto and another large body.

A collision with another body might also have caused Pluto to be knocked over on its side. Unlike Earth and most of the other planets, which rotate on a nearly vertical axis, Pluto's rotational axis is nearly horizontal, so that the planet appears to rotate like a rotisserie chicken. Uranus is the only other planet with such a sideways rotation. Pluto makes a complete rotation every 6.39 days.

The Smallest Planet

In addition to being the outermost planet in the solar system, Pluto is also the smallest. At 1,468 miles (2,370 kilometers) in diameter, Pluto is even smaller than six planetary moons—including Earth's own Moon and some of Jupiter's and Saturn's satellites. Pluto's small size makes even Mercury, the next largest planet, look large by comparison since tiny Pluto is less than half the size of Mercury. It is only 18 percent of the size of Earth and only three-quarters the size of our Moon. Charon, Pluto's only satellite, is even smaller, only about half the size of Pluto.

Density, Surface, and Core

Despite Pluto's small size, scientists think that its density, surface, and core are similar to those of other planets. The planet is relatively dense, made of about 70 percent rock and 30 percent ice. Scientists think that most of the ice on Pluto is water based but that other ice is made of frozen gases such as nitrogen, methane, and carbon monoxide. Because of Pluto's odd oval-shaped orbit, its surface probably changes as the planet gets closer to the Sun. Astronomers believe that when Pluto nears the Sun, some of the surface ice evaporates enough to create a thin atmosphere. Then, as the planet moves away from the Sun, most of the atmosphere will freeze again and fall to the surface in a rare snowfall. "If you're a Plutonian," planetary researcher Richard Binzel has said, "you get snowed on just once a Pluto year, which lasts for [more than] 248 of our years."[2]

Most of the information we have about Pluto's surface has come to us from the powerful Hubble Space Telescope in orbit around Earth. Pluto used to be just a faint blob to astronomers using even the most powerful Earth-based telescopes. In the 1990s, however, Hubble sent back much clearer images, revealing a blotchy surface with dark and light areas. The images also showed that Pluto has large ice caps at its north and south poles,

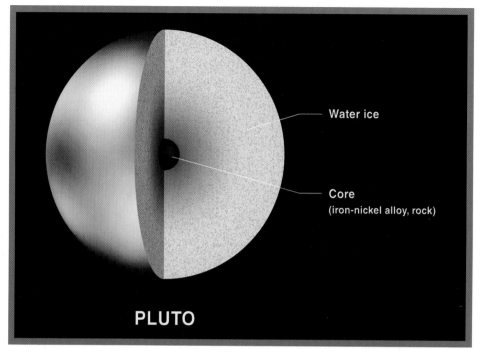

Water ice

Core
(iron-nickel alloy, rock)

PLUTO

Scientists are still not sure what Pluto is made of, but they do know that the planet's surface is covered in ice.

probably made of frozen methane gas, with darker bands circling the equator. Some believe the lighter sections are frozen gases and other icy materials, while the dark sections might be exposed rock. Others think the dark sections are the result of chemical reactions within the ice. Generally, it is thought that Pluto has a reddish color, while Charon is mostly gray.

Because Pluto is so far away, exact measurements of the planet's surface temperature have never been taken. But at 3.7 billion miles (5.9 billion kilometers) from the heating rays of the Sun, Pluto is surely freezing cold. Some estimate that Pluto has a surface temperature of at least −350°F (−212°C). The darker areas might be a few degrees warmer, scientists say—but the planet is still far too cold to sustain life as we know it. Sunlight takes

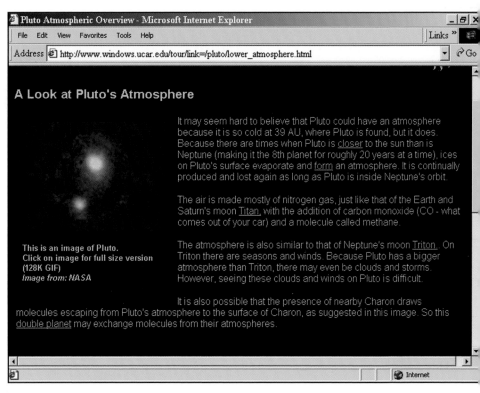

A Look at Pluto's Atmosphere

It may seem hard to believe that Pluto could have an atmosphere because it is so cold at 39 AU, where Pluto is found, but it does. Because there are times when Pluto is closer to the sun than is Neptune (making it the 8th planet for roughly 20 years at a time), ices on Pluto's surface evaporate and form an atmosphere. It is continually produced and lost again as long as Pluto is inside Neptune's orbit.

The air is made mostly of nitrogen gas, just like that of the Earth and Saturn's moon Titan, with the addition of carbon monoxide (CO - what comes out of your car) and a molecule called methane.

This is an image of Pluto.
Click on image for full size version
(128K GIF)
Image from: NASA

The atmosphere is also similar to that of Neptune's moon Triton. On Triton there are seasons and winds. Because Pluto has a bigger atmosphere than Triton, there may even be clouds and storms. However, seeing these clouds and winds on Pluto is difficult.

It is also possible that the presence of nearby Charon draws molecules escaping from Pluto's atmosphere to the surface of Charon, as suggested in this image. So this double planet may exchange molecules from their atmospheres.

▲ *Little is known of Pluto's atmosphere, although scientists believe it is composed primarily of nitrogen.*

nearly seven hours to reach Pluto, where its strength is only a tiny fraction of sunlight's strength on Earth.

▷ Pluto's Atmosphere

Astronomers were not even sure that Pluto had an atmosphere until 1988, when Pluto passed in front of a star. Nitrogen probably makes up most of the atmosphere. There may also be methane, carbon monoxide, and ethane. The great contrasts in temperature between the planet's light and dark regions may cause the incredibly strong winds near the planet's surface. There may also be a low layer of haze covering the planet, like the smog found on Saturn's moon Titan and Neptune's moon Triton.[3]

Chapter 3 ▶

Pluto's Strange Spins and Turns

Our solar system is one of extremes. It contains massive gas giants—Jupiter, Saturn, Uranus, and Neptune, the outer planets— and smaller, rocky terrestrial planets—Mercury, Venus, Earth, and Mars, the inner planets. Some planets are scorching hot, while others are icy and cold. Some of their orbits are nearly circular, while others, like Pluto, are elliptical, or oval. All the planets circle the Sun in the same counterclockwise direction, with most orbits lying on the same plane as the Sun's equator.

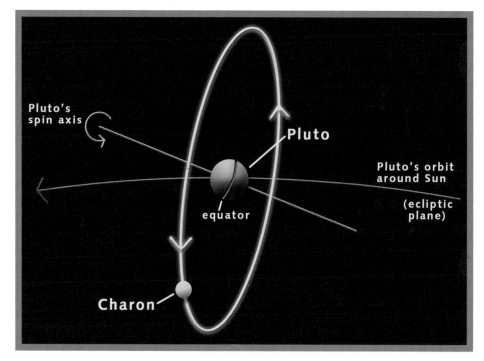

△ Pluto and Uranus are the only planets in the solar system to rotate on their sides. Pluto makes a complete rotation every 6.39 days.

Each orbit lies inside the next one, like the ripples that appear in a pond after a stone is thrown in. And as the planets orbit the Sun, most are rotating on their axes in a mostly vertical position. Pluto's rotation and revolutions are different.

Spinning Sideways

As Pluto orbits the Sun, it rotates on its axis, just as Earth and the other planets do. But as Pluto spins, it is tilted sideways. The only other planet that features such an unusual rotation is Uranus, but even that planet is not tilted at as great an angle as Pluto is. As Pluto spins sideways, the planet experiences night and day. But a day on Pluto is more like a week on Earth: It takes Pluto six days, nine hours, and seventeen minutes to rotate once on its axis.

Pluto's Strange Orbit

But even stranger than the way Pluto rotates is the path it takes to travel around the Sun. Pluto has the strangest orbit of all the planets in the solar system. Unlike all the other planets, which trace around mostly circular flat orbits, one after the other like tree rings, Pluto's orbit is tipped over at a 17-degree angle from the orbital plane, known as the plane of the ecliptic. The orbit is also elongated, as if someone were stretching it out like a piece of clay. Pluto moves both well above and much below the plane where other planets orbit the Sun.

In and Out of Neptune

It takes Pluto nearly 249 years to revolve around the Sun. For nearly twenty of those years, Pluto's highly elliptical orbit actually slips inside Neptune's orbit, so that the ninth planet actually becomes the eighth. Even though the two planets' orbits overlap at Pluto's perihelion point, when it is closest to the Sun, there is no risk of a collision. Neptune always crosses Pluto's orbit when Pluto is at aphelion, its farthest point from the Sun. The two planets also

Sedna
800-1100 miles
in diameter

Quaoar
(800 miles)

Pluto
(1400 miles)

Moon
(2100 miles)

Earth
(8000 miles)

▲ *Sedna, a planetoid close in size to Pluto but three times farther from Earth than Pluto is, was discovered in 2004. Here, Sedna is compared in size to Quaoar, Pluto, Earth's Moon, and Earth.*

do not cross paths because they are not orbiting in the same plane. Pluto will not pass inside Neptune's orbit again until the year 2227—when it will become the eighth planet from the Sun.

So far, astronomers have not settled on one theory for Pluto's odd orbit. Some believe that Pluto was once a moon of Neptune, similar to its largest satellites, Triton and Nereid. Like Pluto, these moons also have strange orbits. Triton revolves around Neptune in a retrograde, or backward, motion. Unlike most planetary bodies, which move around their hosts in a counterclockwise motion, Triton is moving clockwise. Nereid has an elliptical, inclined orbit, much like Pluto's. Some astronomers say that a massive

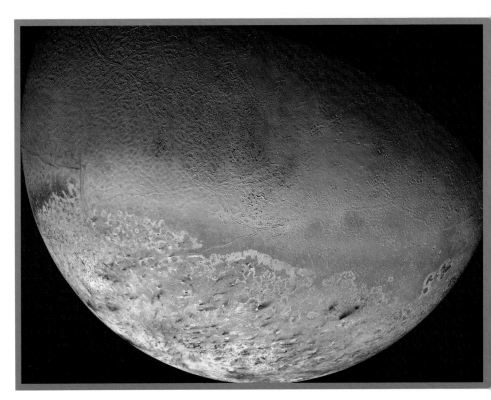

△ *Neptune's moon Triton. Some scientists think that a collision with another plant might have caused both Triton's backward orbit and Pluto's tilted orbit.*

interplanetary collision might have knocked Pluto out of its orbit around Neptune and into its present tilted orbit around the Sun. This same collision might also have knocked Triton into its backward orbit and also created Pluto's moon, Charon. To this day, Neptune's and Pluto's orbits are locked into a mathematical pattern. For every three times Neptune orbits the Sun, Pluto travels around the Sun exactly twice.

Pluto's Moon

For many years, Pluto was seen as nothing more than a distant fuzz ball, even through the most powerful telescopes. As technology improved, however, astronomers noticed that Pluto seemed to bulge out on one side. Even more mysterious, the bulge seemed to change position. On June 22, 1978, astronomer James Christy came to a startling conclusion.

Christy, working at the United States Naval Observatory in Flagstaff, Arizona, had been comparing telescope images to measure Pluto's orbit. To do this, he had to track the planet's motion

▲ Astronomer James Christy (foreground), who discovered Pluto's moon, Charon, in 1978, is pictured at the United States Naval Observatory in Flagstaff, Arizona, with fellow USNO astronomer Robert Harrington.

against the background field of stars. As he tracked Pluto, he noticed the strange bump, which appeared to change positions on Pluto's surface. Soon, Christy concluded that the moving bump was actually an orbiting moon. Christy named the moon Charon, which had a mythological tie to Pluto. In Greek mythology, Charon was the boatman who ferried the souls of the dead across the river Styx to the underworld ruled by Pluto. On a more personal note, *Charon* also sounded like *Charlene,* the name of Christy's wife—who was known informally as Char.[1]

Because no telescopes were powerful enough to show Pluto and Charon as separate bodies, some were skeptical about Christy's discovery. One scientist even wondered whether the bump was just an extremely large mountain on Pluto's surface. It would be years before Charon was officially accepted as a separate moon of Pluto. By then, however, Pluto's very designation as a planet would be questioned.

Charon's Origins

If information about Pluto's origins is sketchy, we know even less about how Charon was formed. Many hold to the belief that Pluto and Charon were created in some interplanetary collision, which also knocked the pair into their present path. Others believe that Pluto, as a rapidly revolving new planet, might have shed enough material to form a moon. Still others think that Pluto and Charon formed together out of the solar nebula as a pair, forever linked in space.

The Largest Satellite

Charon is roughly 740 miles (1,190 kilometers) in diameter, about half the size of Pluto. This makes Charon the largest satellite in proportion to its host planet of any planet in the solar system. Earth's Moon is the second largest, with a diameter one-quarter that of Earth. The giant moons of Jupiter and Saturn, which measure more than 3,000 miles (4,827 kilometers) across, are much larger

An artist's conception of the New Horizons spacecraft, which is scheduled to begin its mission to Pluto in 2006.

than Charon, but they are dwarfed by their giant host planets—the largest planets in the solar system. Regardless of their origins, Pluto and Charon are now so closely linked that the two are often referred to as a binary planet or a double planet.

"Charon is so big, relative to Pluto's size, that the two bodies constitute a double planet," said Alan Stern, a planetary scientist at the Southwest Research Institute in Boulder, Colorado, who will be the principal investigator of New Horizons, a mission to Pluto and Charon scheduled to launch in 2006. "There's no other pair quite like them in the solar system. But we think when we get to study them close up, we'll find parallels to binary stars."[2]

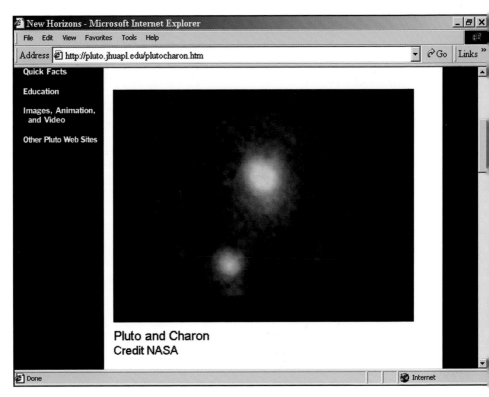

New Horizons - Microsoft Internet Explorer

File   Edit   View   Favorites   Tools   Help

Address http://pluto.jhuapl.edu/plutocharon.htm   Go   Links

Quick Facts

Education

Images, Animation,
  and Video

Other Pluto Web Sites

Pluto and Charon
Credit NASA

Done   Internet

▲ *A rare image of Pluto, top, and Charon, bottom, was captured by the Hubble.*

Astronomers believe that Pluto and Charon exchange material and affect each other's orbital motions. Pluto and Charon, although 12,177 miles (19,593 kilometers) apart, circle each other around a center of gravity located in the space between the two bodies. In most planet-moon systems, such as that of Earth and its Moon, the center of gravity exists in the larger planet.

Rotation and Orbit

Pluto and Charon are locked into an interesting and unchanging formation in space. They rotate on their axes and orbit their hosts at the exact same rate, which is called synchronous rotation and revolution. This means that Pluto and Charon always show the same face toward each other, just as our Moon always shows the same face to Earth. If life-forms could survive on the side of Pluto that never faced Charon, those life-forms would never even know that Pluto had a moon.

To make it easier to understand, some people compare Pluto and Charon to a weight-lifting dumbbell, with the weight on one end twice as large as the other. If this dumbbell were tossed into orbit by a fantasy giant, the two end weights would be forever locked into position. (For this to happen with Earth and its Moon, Earth would have to be pulled into a rhythm with the Moon's orbit, rotating once every 28 days, instead of once every 24 hours. The Moon would have to be much larger and much closer to exert this kind of gravitational pull on Earth—as Charon does with Pluto.)

Recent images captured by the Hubble Space Telescope have revealed a surprising fact about Charon: Charon's orbit is not perfectly circular, as scientists previously thought. Instead, Charon has an elliptical orbit, which astronomers say is surprising, given how perfectly synchronized Pluto and Charon are. Like the common theories about Pluto's orbit, it is believed that a relatively recent collision might have knocked Charon into its slightly off-kilter path.

▶ Surface and Core

Astronomers believe that Charon's structure is very similar to Pluto's, but with a smaller core relative to the moon's size. Charon has a lower density than Pluto, which means that it is likely to have a higher proportion of ice. Unlike Pluto, Charon does not appear to have frozen methane on its surface—only water ice has been found so far. However, scientists are not ruling out that Charon's surface might also contain a small percentage of frozen methane, nitrogen, and carbon monoxide. In addition, some say that Charon's darker color might be due to the presence of some kind of dirt, made of yet-undiscovered organic materials.

▲ *An artist's idea of what Pluto, at right, and Charon, its moon, might look like.*

▷ Mutual Events

Between 1985 and 1990, astronomers realized they had great luck when it came to studying Charon. During that brief five-year period, Charon and Pluto moved in front of each other when astronomers viewed the pair from Earth. This allowed astronomers to monitor both the combined and individual brightness of the objects, which offered clues to their surface materials, reflectivity, and color. Pluto appears much darker when Charon passes in front of it, a combination of Charon's grayish color and the shadow it casts on Pluto.

Known as "mutual events," these movements occur only twice during Pluto's nearly 249-year orbit around the Sun. If Charon had been discovered only fifteen years later, scientists would have had to wait until the twenty-second century for this phenomenon to occur again.

Chapter 5 ▶

The Final Frontier Explored

Pluto is so far away and so difficult to see, even with the world's most powerful telescopes, that sending a spacecraft there was basically unthinkable until recently. To us on Earth, Pluto appears about four thousand times dimmer than the faintest star that we can make out with the naked eye. Pluto's discoverer, Clyde Tombaugh, once noted the distance when a planetary

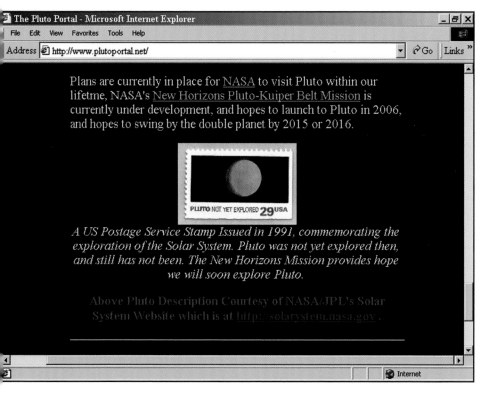

The Pluto Portal - Microsoft Internet Explorer

File   Edit   View   Favorites   Tools   Help

Address   http://www.plutoportal.net/   Go   Links

Plans are currently in place for NASA to visit Pluto within our lifetme, NASA's New Horizons Pluto-Kuiper Belt Mission is currently under development, and hopes to launch to Pluto in 2006, and hopes to swing by the double planet by 2015 or 2016.

PLUTO NOT YET EXPLORED **29**USA

A US Postage Service Stamp Issued in 1991, commemorating the exploration of the Solar System. Pluto was not yet explored then, and still has not been. The New Horizons Mission provides hope we will soon explore Pluto.

Above Pluto Description Courtesy of NASA/JPL's Solar System Website which is at http://solarsystem.nasa.gov.

△ The United States Postal Service unwittingly helped speed up plans to explore Pluto, the planet "not yet explored," with this commemorative stamp, issued in 1991.

researcher asked him about a possible mission to Pluto. "I told him he was welcome to it," Tombaugh recalled, "though he's got to go one long, cold trip."[1]

In 1991, however, the United States Postal Service unknowingly planted the seed of exploration with a new series of postage stamps. The series depicted all the planets and the spacecraft that had explored them—including Mars and *Viking*, Jupiter and *Pioneer*, and Neptune and *Voyager*, among others. On the Pluto stamp, the small, lonely-looking planet was suspended in a black sky above the phrase "Pluto Not Yet Explored." The stamp "bothered me a lot," said Robert Staehle, a scientist at the California Institute of Technology's Jet Propulsion Laboratory, who immediately began pushing for a mission to Pluto.[2]

Although Pluto has not yet been explored, it has certainly been studied. Like a scavenger hunt in which one clue leads to another, the discovery of Pluto came about only after several previous findings. First, English astronomer William Herschel stumbled across Uranus in 1781. With this discovery, Herschel had doubled the known size of the solar system from less than a billion miles in length—the distance of Saturn from the Sun—to about 2 billion miles. In the years that followed, astronomers noticed the strange tugging on Uranus's orbit, suggesting that another planet lay beyond it. This in turn led to the discovery of Neptune in 1846 by three men, individually. Then, finally, these findings spurred Percival Lowell's quest to find Planet X at the turn of the twentieth century, which led to Clyde Tombaugh finding Pluto in 1930.

"When I made the Pluto discovery," Tombaugh said, "only a few individuals dreamed of going to the planets—and even we didn't expect to see this happen in our lifetime."[3]

▷ Leaps and Bounds

The planetary speck that Tombaugh saw through his telescope was far from clear, however. For four decades, details about Pluto's

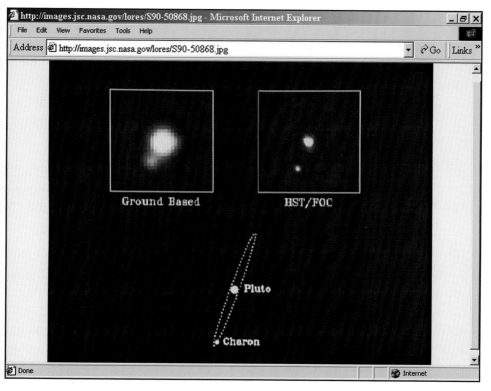

http://images.jsc.nasa.gov/lores/S90-50868.jpg - Microsoft Internet Explorer

File   Edit   View   Favorites   Tools   Help

Address http://images.jsc.nasa.gov/lores/S90-50868.jpg   Go   Links

Ground Based   HST/FOC

Pluto

Charon

Done   Internet

△ *Three in one: The image of Pluto and Charon on the left is one of the best ground-based photographs we have of the "double planet." It was taken by a telescope in Hawaii. The image to its right was captured by the Hubble, and the diagram beneath shows Charon's orbit around Pluto.*

surface and composition were few and far between. At most, the world's most powerful telescopes could make out only Pluto's vaguely red color and the fact that it had dark and light blotches. By tracking the blotches as they appeared and disappeared from view, astronomers figured out Pluto's 6.39-day rotational period.

In the 1970s, however, the study of Pluto advanced by leaps and bounds. In 1976, infrared detectors had discovered that Pluto was covered with frozen methane. The discovery was considered a triumph for the modern science of spectroscopy, which studies the frequency of the light given off or absorbed by various atoms and molecules. These frequencies are called "spectral lines."

If it were not for the images of Pluto taken by cameras aboard the Hubble Space Telescope, we would have even fewer pictures of the ninth planet than we do now.

By studying the sunlight reflected from Pluto's surface, scientists could isolate the spectral lines of methane. Until that point, only water-based ice and frozen carbon dioxide had been discovered in the solar system. Only two years later, this discovery was followed by James Christy's discovery of Pluto's moon, Charon.

But it was not until the Hubble Space Telescope photographs, sent back in the 1990s, that astronomers had their clearest images of Pluto. Hubble is the first space-based telescope, now in orbit around Earth. A space-based telescope provides much clearer images than those captured by telescopes on Earth because there is no interference from Earth's relatively thick atmosphere. In the clarity of space, Hubble allowed researchers to more accurately measure Pluto's and Charon's densities and map Pluto's surface.

For the first time, astronomers could map about a dozen distinctive areas on Pluto's surface, with some stretching more than 620 miles (998 kilometers) across. These sections included a ragged polar ice cap, clusters of bright and dark spots, and an intriguing linear marking. Some believe that the marking could be an ejecta ray from a large crater. Ejecta rays are formed when dirt and debris are displaced by a crater-causing impact. Many such rays are visible around our Moon's craters.

The Last Planet to Be Explored

In recent years, astronomers have realized that there is much to gain from an exploratory mission to Pluto. Scientists wonder whether Pluto might have volcanoes, as Neptune's moon Triton does, or whether its surface features vary widely, like those on Mars. Like the gas giants in the outer solar system, Pluto and Charon might also be circled by small satellites that have so far escaped detection. Pluto might even have a ring around it! Recent explorations have discovered rings around every planet from Jupiter to Neptune.

By the early 1990s, the National Aeronautics and Space Administration (NASA) had developed a low-cost mission—called the Pluto Fast Flyby—to study the planet up close. As designed, the Flyby would involve two twin spacecraft, which would reach Pluto within a year of each other. By sending back two different batches of information, the Flyby spacecraft would offer much-sought-after answers to Pluto's mysteries. In the worst-case scenario, the second craft would act as a backup if the first mission failed.

Eventually, the project was expanded to include studies of Charon and the Kuiper Belt. To reflect the change, the project was renamed the Pluto-Kuiper Express. Specific goals included recording the geology of Pluto and Charon, mapping Pluto's surface, and figuring out the composition of Pluto's atmosphere. Timing for the mission was important. NASA hoped to launch the mission by the end of the 1990s, to take advantage of the short period when Pluto's surface was warm enough to support a thin atmosphere. If the mission took too long, Pluto would experience its rare snowfall, blanketing the surface and making data-gathering difficult. Unfortunately, budget cuts at NASA forced the space agency to quickly scrap the Pluto-Kuiper Express mission.

Excitement on the Horizon

But NASA is developing a new mission to explore Pluto and the Kuiper Belt. This mission, called New Horizons: Shedding

Scientists are hopeful that NASA's New Horizons mission to Pluto and beyond will shed light on the last frontier of the solar system.

Light on Frontier Worlds, involves a less expensive spacecraft. The mission, scheduled to launch on January 11, 2006, plans to use Jupiter's gravity as a slingshot by flying by Jupiter in March 2007. That gravity assist will allow the spacecraft to reach Pluto between November 2016 and July 2017 and make a flyby of the Kuiper Belt between 2018 and 2022. If the project is delayed, which could happen if there are more budget cuts, the mission could still launch and avoid Jupiter altogether, although it would take longer to reach Pluto. But time is running out. By the year 2040, Pluto will be farther away along its elliptical orbit, making it harder to reach and explore.

The New Horizons project includes a special instrument called an ultraviolet spectrometer—better known to NASA scientists as "Alice." Alice's main job is to detect what Pluto's atmosphere is made of and to search for an atmosphere around Charon. Also on board will be the Solar Wind Around Pluto (SWAP) instrument. The SWAP device is designed to measure the interactions between Pluto, Charon, and the solar wind, which is the unending stream of particles flowing out from the Sun. This information will help researchers to understand some of the processes that affect the outer solar system.

A Search for the Unexpected

Pluto and the Kuiper Belt present the last frontier in the exploration of our solar system. Scientists hope that the New Horizons mission will not only answer questions about this part of space but will also yield clues to the solar system's beginnings. "Visiting Pluto and other Kuiper Belt objects would be like visiting a deep freeze containing samples of the most ancient material in our solar system, the stuff that all the other planets including Earth were made of," said Dr. Colleen Hartman, a space exploration official with NASA, when the New Horizons project was announced. "But the most exciting thing about going to an unexplored planet is what we may find there that we're not expecting."[4]

The mission's principal investigator, Alan Stern, likens this new frontier in exploration to the "Wild West." In an interview with NASA in which Stern was asked why we need to send a spacecraft to Pluto and the Kuiper Belt, the planetary scientist, who has studied the outer solar system for twenty-two years, had this answer.

> We're in the space exploration business and the outer solar system is a wild, wooly place. We haven't explored it very well. Pluto and the Kuiper Belt have been just ranked by our once-every-ten-years decadal survey to be the highest priority for exploration in the solar system. That's not by our group,

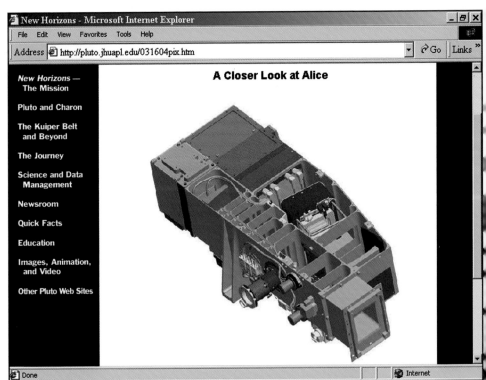

The New Horizons spacecraft will feature an ultraviolet spectrometer nicknamed Alice, pictured, and a digital imager named Ralph—a nod to two of the main characters from The Honeymooners television series.

http://www.solarviews.com/raw/art/kuiperbelt.jpg - Microsoft Internet Explorer

File   Edit   View   Favorites   Tools   Help   Links »

Address 🗎 http://www.solarviews.com/raw/art/kuiperbelt.jpg   🕐 Go

🌐 Internet

▲ *A strange, icy, and mostly mysterious world is captured in this artist's view of the Kuiper Belt.*

but an independent panel from the National Academy of Sciences. It's No. 1 on the runway for making progress toward understanding the birth of the solar system.[5]

This "primitive" region of the solar system is just waiting to be explored. For astronomers, Pluto's mysteries are just waiting to be solved. And according to Stern, it cannot happen too soon . . . "because we know so little, we have so much to gain."[6]

aphelion—A celestial body's farthest position from the Sun.

asteroids—Rocky space objects; most orbit the Sun in a belt between Mars and Jupiter.

axis—An imaginary straight line around which an object, such as a planet, spins, or rotates.

ethane—A colorless, odorless gaseous compound made of carbon and hydrogen.

gas giants—The collective name given to Jupiter, Saturn, Uranus, and Neptune, the four outer planets of the solar system, because of their size and gaseous compositions.

Kuiper Belt—A region of icy objects that lies beyond Neptune.

Kuiper Belt Objects (KBOs)—The icy objects that make up the Kuiper Belt.

nebula—A cloud of gas and dust in which a star is born.

parameters—A set of properties that characterizes something.

perihelion—A celestial body's closest position to the Sun.

reflectivity—The amount of light that an object reflects.

solar wind—A continuous stream of charged particles released from the Sun.

terrestrial—Earth-like; the four inner planets, Mercury, Venus, Earth, and Mars, are known as the terrestrial planets because they have similar rocky compositions.

Chapter Notes

Chapter 1. The Man Who Found Planet X

1. William Sheehan, *Worlds in the Sky: Planetary Discovery From Earliest Times Through Voyager and Magellan* (Tucson: The University of Arizona Press, 1992), p. 191.

2. Jay M. Pasachoff and Donald H. Menzel, *Peterson Field Guides: Stars and Planets* (Boston: Houghton Mifflin Co., 1997), p. 400.

3. James Trefil, "The Astronomer Who Discovered Pluto in 1930 Still Keeps an Eye on the Sky from His Backyard in New Mexico," *Smithsonian,* vol. 22, no. 2, May 1991, p. 32.

4. Sheehan, p. 194.

5. New Mexico State University, Press Release, "Clyde Tombaugh, Discoverer of Pluto, Dies," January 19, 1997, <http://www.klx.com/clyde/nmsu.html> (January 10, 2005).

6. National Aeronautics and Space Administration, Solar System Exploration, News Archive, "Good News for Pluto," November 10, 2004, reprinted from University of Arizona press release, <http://solarsystem.nasa.gov/news/display.cfm?News_ID=10125> (December 15, 2004).

7. Ibid.

Chapter 2. The Most Distant Planet

1. Jay M. Pasachoff and Donald H. Menzel, *Peterson Field Guides: Stars and Planets* (Boston: Houghton Mifflin Co., 1997), p. 400.

2. Dava Sobel, "The Last World: Pluto," *Discover,* vol. 14, no. 5, May 1993, p. 68.

3. Sir Patrick Moore, *Astronomy Encyclopedia* (New York: Oxford University Press, 2002), p. 315.

Chapter 4. Pluto's Moon

1. Dava Sobel, "The Last World: Pluto," *Discover,* vol. 14, no. 5, May 1993, p. 68.

2. Ibid.

Chapter 5. The Final Frontier Explored

1. Dava Sobel, "The Last World: Pluto," *Discover,* vol. 14, no. 5, May 1993, p. 68.

2. Ibid.

3. Ibid.

4. National Aeronautics and Space Administration, NASA press release, "NASA Selects Pluto-Kuiper Belt Mission for Phase B Study," November 29, 2001, <nssdc.gsfc.nasa.gov/planetary/text/pluto_pr_20011129.txt> (December 15, 2004).

5. National Aeronautics and Space Administration, Solar System Exploration, Q & A With Alan Stern, "Pushing the Envelope on the Solar System's 'Wild West' Frontiers," n.d., <http://solarsystem.nasa.gov/people/profile.cfm?Code=SternA> (December 15, 2004).

6. Ibid.

Further Reading

Asimov, Isaac. *Pluto and Charon*. Milwaukee, Wis.: Gareth Stevens Publishing, 2002.

Cole, Michael D. *Pluto—The Ninth Planet*. Berkeley Heights, N.J.: Enslow Publishers, Inc., 2002.

Hayhurst, Chris. *Pluto*. New York: Rosen Publishing Group, 2004.

Littmann, Mark. *Planets Beyond: Discovering the Outer Solar System*. New York: Dover Publications, 2004.

Miller, Ron. *Mercury and Pluto*. Brookfield, Conn.: Twenty-First Century Books, 2003.

Rau, Dana Meachen. *Pluto*. Minneapolis: Compass Point Books, 2003.

Ride, Sally, and Tam O'Shaughnessy. *Exploring Our Solar System*. New York: Crown Publishers, 2002.

Stefoff, Rebecca. *Pluto*. New York: Benchmark Books, 2003.

Stern, Alan, and Jacqueline Mitton. *Pluto and Charon: Ice Worlds on the Ragged Edge of the Solar System*. New York: Wiley, 1998.

Tocci, Salvatore. *A Look at Pluto*. New York: Franklin Watts, 2003.

Wetterer, Margaret K. *Clyde Tombaugh and the Search for Planet X*. Minneapolis: Carolrhoda Books, 1996.

Whitehouse, Patricia. *The Planets*. Chicago: Heinemann Library, 2005.